Heart O' Scotland
A Kid's Guide To Pitlochry, Scotland

Photography by John D. Weigand
Poetry by Penelope Dyan

Bellissima Publishing, LLC
Jamul, California
www.bellissimapublishing.com

Copyright © 2014 by Penny D. Weigand and John D. Weigand

All rights reserved. No part of this book may be reproduced or transmitted in any form or by any means, electronic or mechanical, including photocopying, recording, or by any other means, or by any information or storage retrieval system, without permission from the publisher.

ISBN 978-1-61477-137-1
First Edition

"A gude beginning maks a gude ending."
Meaning:
"A good beginning makes a good ending."

"If ye like the nut, crack it."
Meaning:
"He that would eat the kernel must crack the nut."

Scottish Proverbs

Heart O' Scotland
Bellissima Publishing, LLC

Introduction

Pitlochry is located in th heart of Scotland, a quaint, old town that is very friendly and lots of fun for kids. This is because people here seem to have a sense of humor, shopping is good, and there is a lot to see and do, especially if your family likes to go hiking in the beautiful hillside highlands. And if you really don't fancy a walk in the heather, this place is still both amusing and fun! It's a Victorian town that became a tourist resort when Queen Victoria visited it in 1842. And the arrival of the railway in 1863 solidified its stature. (Our author and photographer came by rail, which is a fun experience in and of itself!)

Peek through the camera lens of John D. Weigand as he and our author, Penelope Dyan, show you a bit of what you might see when you go to this wonderful, small burgh. Practice your reading skills through word recognition, repetition and rhyme as you vicariously explore with Penelope Dyan, an award winning author, attorney and former teacher, and photographer, John D. Weigand. Then have even more fun with the music video on the Bellissimavideo YouTube Channel that goes along with this book (a perfectly sized book, with extra large print for little eyes to easily see and read.) And then learn even more! Let your young imagination go wild! That's what an imagination is supposed to do!

Heart O' Scotland
Bellissima Publishing, LLC

Heart O' Scotland
A Kid's Guide To Pitlochry, Scotland

Photography by John D. Weigand
Poetry by Penelope Dyan

There is a bakery in Pitlochry, where you can get something to eat, something yummy, something sweet.

When you are walking over to there,
you might catch the eye
of a teddy bear.
Or you might just catch
the eyes of two,
looking back through a shop window.
and straight at you!

Your Mom laughs and says,
"Look there is a kilt
and a purse for dad!
I wonder how he would look,
dressed in a kilt of plaid."
Then she adds, "If he bought one,
then we could find out
exactly what goes under there,
and whether Scottish men
wear underwear!"

Then dad says,
"Mom, you're in luck!
I can buy YOU a wooden duck!"
Of course, the purse is what
she'd rather choose,
over a duck that wears
blue with white polka dotted shoes!
But then, if you asked me, I'd say
she could buy the whole family of three!
(I'd tell her the one that I liked BEST
was the ducky that wore
the plaid buttoned down vest.)

There is a water wheel.
It's in front of a restaurant
where you can get a good meal!

You all walk down the quiet street.
The pavement dances
beneath your feet.

In the distance the hills look red.
Mom reminds you,
"Soon it will be time for bed!"

The entire town seems quiet and still.
You watch a Scotsman walk up a hill.

And then some 'big wheels'
from down the street bound.
The driver honks his horn loudly,
and makes a great BIG sound!

Then you see the sign.
Could this POSSIBLY be true?
Mom says, "I wouldn't go
looking in THERE if I were YOU!"

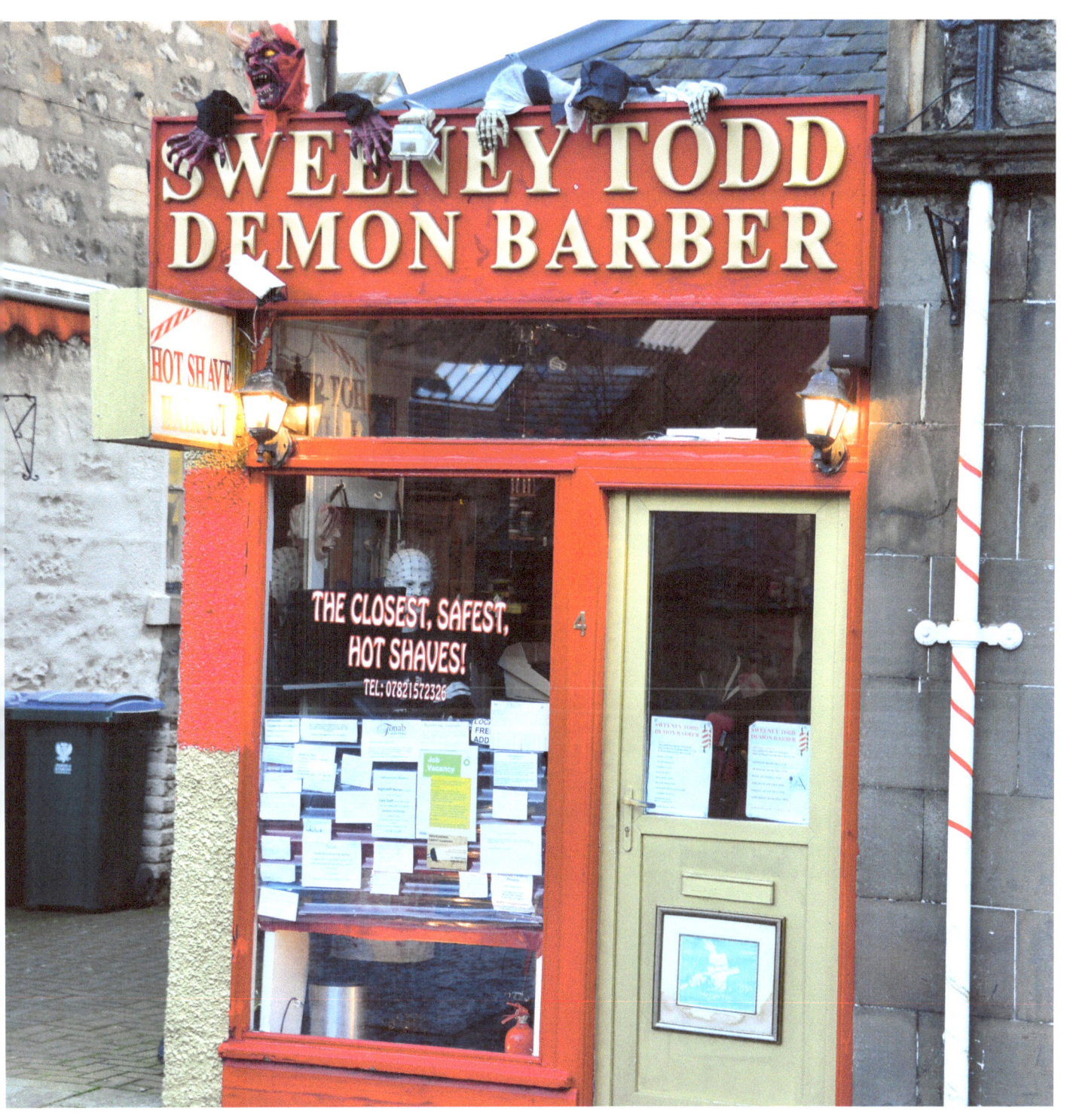

Then through a window
you take a peek inside.
And from the gory truth,
you CANNOT hide.
If you go into THIS place
they MIGHT take your brains
right out of your head,
and then serve them for dinner,
with mashed peas and white bread!

Perhaps it's time to get moving along.
And as you walk you can sing a song.
And then it will ALL disappear,
the evil and the dread,
that at Sweeney Todd's Barber Shop
got into your small head.
Mom says,
"I told you NOT to look inside!
From imagination you cannot hide."
And then you laugh at all that stuff,
because as to thinking about it,
you have NOW had ENOUGH!
And as you later lay in your hotel bed,
thoughts of beautiful heather
(instead) fill your head.

"When ae door steeks anither opens."
Meaning:
"When one door closes another opens."

A Scottish Proverb